CAT
T·A·L·E·S

Edited by **Suzanne Beilenson**

Design by
Scharr Design

PETER PAUPER PRESS, INC.
WHITE PLAINS   NEW YORK

For Tante Martha

Copyright © 1992
Peter Pauper Press, Inc.
202 Mamaroneck Avenue
White Plains, NY 10601
All rights reserved
ISBN 0-88088-074-0
Printed in Singapore
7   6   5   4   3   2   1

CONTENTS

A LITTLE HISTORY
OF FELINES

*H*ERE, KITTY KITTY! Here, Kitty Kitty! For thousands of years, human beings have been coaxing and cajoling—with differing degrees of success—that splendid and singular creature known as the cat.

The ancient Egyptians were the first to fall under the cat's sublime spell. They worshiped the cat in the form of the goddess *Bast,* who had the head of a cat but the body of a human; the killing of a cat was punishable by death. Pilgrims often traveled to the Temple of Bast to place mummified cats in its sanctuary, along with mummified rice and milk for the feline hereafter. When a cat died, Egyptians mourned the loss by shaving off their eyebrows. Tombs of Egyptian royalty often contained mummified cats beside the mummies of their royal masters.

Sanskrit writings reveal the cat's presence in India, and in China there is evidence that Confucius kept a cat—perhaps inspiring all his wise sayings! The cities of Carthage and Alexandria in olden times had cat populations of over 100,000.

Phoenician traders are believed to have brought the domesticated Egyptian cat to Britain around 900 B.C. The Romans considered the cat a symbol of liberty, and it followed then into Europe as the Roman Empire expanded. A European domesticated breed eventually developed from the inbreeding of the Egyptian variety with European wild cats, but was destined to have a much more turbulent history than its Egyptian cousin.

In about 600 A.D. the Prophet Muhammad preached to the multitudes while holding a cat in his arms.

Throughout the Middle Ages, European cats, especially black ones, became associated with black magic and witches. Often cats were thought to be witches in disguise, or to be vested with the spirit of Satan that could cause harm to people while they slept. The cat thus became a dreaded creature.

It is thus not surprising that until the 17th Century the French burned thousands of cats to safeguard the people from witches. King Louis XIII put a stop to it, but in the 1730's cats were ritually massacred as a social protest against the state of affairs in Paris at the time. The French, however, were not the only perpetrators. By the 18th Century, the cat was no longer a prized possession to the

British either. A visitor to the Tower of London's menageries could either pay a fee or furnish a cat to be fed to the lions.

By the 1870's, though, the illustrious cat had regained its status with the Europeans. The English relied on cats to rid their country of rodents. One wealthy squire actually levied a fine (in bushels of corn) on anyone who intentionally killed a cat. In 1871, the first modern cat show was mounted at the famous Crystal Palace in London, and soon it was an annual event. It was followed by a Scottish cat show in Edinburgh in 1875. By 1895, the Americans had caught feline fever and held a full-fledged cat show at Madison Square Garden with more than 200 cats being exhibited. Today, there are over 400 cat shows staged annually throughout the United States.

It seems, at last, that after 4,000 years the cat has finally come full circle. While these days we may not rank the cat with the gods (as the Egyptians did), it is fair to say that cat lovers abound everywhere.

We hope you and your feline friends enjoy our catty concoction of Dear Tabby's, cat words, famous felines, superstitions, cats in art and literature, quotes, and poems. And don't forget to place your kitty's favorite photo in the frame we've provided!

S. B.

M Y   C A T

PLACE
YOUR
CATS
PHOTO
HERE

Dear Tabby,

I am obsessed with a real Feline Fatale. She's gorgeous, and I would do anything to be with her. I've made a few advances, and she acts like she's interested, but then she'll ignore me for days. I'm not sure how much longer I can take these cat-and-mouse games. I'd forget her if I could, but I can't. How can I make her love me?

Signed,
At Cat Woman's
Mercy

Dear At Cat Woman's Mercy,

What are you? A man or a mouse? If you continue to let your feline friend stick her claws in you, you deserve what you get. The sooner you drop her like a bad piece of fish, the better.

Dear Tabby,

I'm a mother of 16, and expecting yet another kitty litter. I love my babies, but I am tuckered out. There just doesn't seem to be time enough in the day to feed them all, clean them all, and take them all to the park. I catnap whenever I can, but it doesn't seem to help. What can I do?

> *Signed,*
> *On My Last Paw*

Dear On My Last Paw,

What you need, my dear, is a vaCATion. So drop the kits at your mother's or hire a sitter. There are lots of great places to relax and unwind. Might I suggest a few? The Catskills, Catalina Island, St. Kitts . . .

D E A R

T A B B Y

Dear Tabby,

My younger sister is driving me up a tree.
Whatever I do, she copycats. If I go for a
lick of milk, she goes for a lick of milk. If I
wear a rhinestone collar, she wears one too.
I've tried everything to get her to stop, but
nothing works. Pretty soon I'm going to
scratch her eyes out. HELP!

Signed,
A Suffering Siamese

Dear Suffering Siamese,

Younger kitties often mimic their older
siblings in an attempt to seem more
mature. Your sister is simply showing
her admiration for you. Don't be so
catty. Spend a little quality time
with her—say, throwing the old ball
of yarn around. She might feel less
ignored, and give you your space.

12

Dear Tabby,

I have soft black hair, glassy green eyes, and a curvaceous figure. Whenever I go out by myself, all of the toms in the neighborhood meow and make catcalls as I pass by. I don't do anything to encourage their remarks, and I wish they would stop. It isn't fair. I can't help the way I look.

> *Signed,*
> *Victim of Desire*

Dear Victim of Desire,

Granted, sometimes it's best just to ignore those terrible toms, but evidently that strategy hasn't worked for you. So quit pussyfooting around. The next time they start in on you, give it right back and tell them to go to Purrrgatory!

CAT·NIP	*Feline love bite*
CAT·WALK	*Pussy prowl*
CAT·TY	*"Meow-Meow"*
CAT·KIN	*Feline family*
POPO·**CAT**·EPETL	*Mexican cat with volcanic temper*
DE·**CAT**·HLON	*Track and field event at Cat Olympics*
HEP·**CAT**	*Katharine's favorite feline*
CAT·TISH	*Four-fifths feline*
CAT·TY-CORNER	*When Tom has Jerry in a jam*

CAT·CALL	*Feline 'fone conversation*
CAT·HODE·RAY TUBE	*Permits Cable TV for pussycats*
CAT·ABOLISM	*Feline blood pressure, digestion, etc.*
CAT·ACLYSM	*Two toms out at night*
CAT·ALYTIC CONVERTER	*Changes a kitten into a cat*
CAT·ALEPSY	*When a cat sleeps 22 hours a day*
CAT·AMOUNT	*Pussy peak overlooking Katmandu*

AT DIC

CAT·ALOG *Cat's diary*

CAT·AMARAN *Boat for the owl and the pussycat*

CAT·SUP *A relish for pet food*

CAT·ATONIC *Feline summer drink*

CAT·EGORY *A horror story about cats*

CAT·ASTROPHY *Award for catching a mouse*

CAT·SKILL *Tabby talent*

CAT·TLE *They say "meow" instead of "moo"*

‌IONARY

CAT·ALYST	*Feline phone book*
CAT·ENATION	*Kitty kingdom*
KITTY HAWK	*Capital of Catenation*
CAT·ARACTS	*Imperfect pupils*
CAT·NAP	*The big sleep*
CAT'S CRADLE	*Love game*
CAT·TAIL	*Kitty legend*
CAT·CHER	*Four-legged baseball player*
KAT·MANDU	*Capital of Nepalese cats*
CAT·ACOMB	*Used with a CATABRUSH*

FAMOUS FELINES

Morris the Cat, the talking cat of advertising fame

Garfield, of the comic strip

Cat in the Hat, courtesy of Dr. Seuss

Pink Panther, immortalized in human form by Peter Sellers

Cowardly Lion, Dorothy's furry friend

Puss in Boots, the sly, boot-wearing cat of the fairy tale

Tony the Tiger, spokescat for Frosted Flakes

Cheshire Cat, Alice's smiling companion

Sylvester, the adversary of the cartoon character Tweetie-Pie

The Sphinx, Egypt's biggest cat

Spike the Wondercat, a Beilenson phenomenon

FAMOUS FELINES

Tigger, the frolicking friend of
    Winnie the Pooh

Cat Stevens, who sang as well as purred

Kitty Dukakis, a political pussycat

Kitty Kelley, a catty biographer

Cat Woman, Batman's purrrrfect crook

Tom, of the cat and mouse duo,
    Tom and Jerry

Felix the Cat, famed cartoon character
    since the 1920's

Heathcliff, the tough little cat of
    the comics

SAYINGS ABOUT CATS

A cat has nine lives.

Ancient peoples were amazed that cats always landed on their feet, even from "impossible" positions. Modern scientists, using high-speed photography, have shown that the spine of the cat is incredibly supple, and that all parts of the cat move in harmony to achieve a landing "on all fours."

Honest as a cat when the cream is out of reach.

People are honest too, unless there is money lying on the street. The saying denotes a person who is not to be trusted.

Even a cat can look at a king.

A citizen has a vote, and the protection of the law, even if he or she is not the president or a powerful figure.

When the cat's away, the mice will play

Just ask the babysitter!

Curiosity killed the cat.

It's dangerous to be *too* curious!

THE MYSTERIOUS KITTY

*W*HEN THE CAT'S AWAY, mice may play, but when the cat's around, mysteries abound! Superstitions have always seemed to trail this reserved and independent creature.

One of the earliest and most famous superstitions is that the cat possesses nine lives. The "nine" is often believed to stem from the religious Trinity—nine being a trinity of trinities, and, therefore, particularly symbolic. The nine lives superstition has led to many unusual behaviors—such as keeping a cat aboard a boat to ward off danger.

Supernatural beliefs about cats often revolve around nighttime. People have throughout history endowed the cat with the ability to see in the dark because its eyes appear to glow at night. (Cats see no better in the dark than the average human, but their eyes do gather and reflect whatever light is available.)

Cats are also associated with the moon. Moon myths arose from a story about the Greek goddess Artemis (later named Diana by the Romans), who, being chased by a monster named Typhon, changed herself into a cat and hid in the moon. Here also lies the basis for the many folk tales of women, and especially witches, metamorphosing into cats.

Even cat hairs are brushed with superstition! In the Ozarks of mid-America, cat hairs can determine whether a girl should accept a proposal of marriage. The young lady simply plucks three hairs from a cat's tail, wraps them in paper, and places them at her front door. If, in the morning, the three hairs appear to form a "Y," she accepts. It they seem to form an "N," she declines.

A cat hair can supposedly also be used to cure ailments. One example is that of using a hair from the tail of a black cat to relieve a swollen eyelid or sty. The hair must be plucked on the first night of a full moon (of course!) and stroked across the ailing lid nine times (of course, again!).

THE ARTISTIC KITTY

*S*INCE THE EGYPTIANS first took a fancy to the feline, artists have been inspired by cats. An Egyptian tomb drawing from approximately 2,600 B.C. is one of the first works of art to feature a cat. Later Egyptians produced sculptures of cats in bronze and other materials.

Cats are a particular favorite of the artists of France and East Asia. The French Impressionist Pierre August Renoir painted his *Girl with a Cat*, Theodore Gericault did *Studies of a Cat* in pencil, and Gustave Courbet is known for his *Woman with a Cat*. The 18th Century Japanese artist Ichiryusai Hiroshige often depicted his feline model in woodblock prints.

Modern American artists from Norman Rockwell to Andrew Wyeth have focused their attention on the cat. Sculptures by Edward F. Hoffman III and Heinz Warneke, and oil paintings such as *Black Panther* by Alice Dineen and *Hot Milk: Waiting for it to Cool* by Elisabeth F. Bonsall are examples.

THE LITERARY KITTY

*A*S THE CAT HAS MADE a strong showing in the art world, so also has the feline graced the pages of literature! Since cats first arrived in Aesop's fables, kitties have been appearing, or disappearing (like Lewis Carroll's Cheshire Cat!), in the literary realm. Among these famous fictional cats are Beatrix Potter's tidy, housekeeping cat Simkins, Edgar Allan Poe's Pluto, Saki's gossipy pussycat Tobermory, Charles Dickens' beastly Lady Jane from *Bleak House,* and, of course, Puss in Boots, the crafty hero of the fairy tale by Perrault.

While perhaps the most famous collection of kitty poems is T. S. Eliot's *Old Possum's Book of Practical Cats,* there are heaps of other verses featuring cats, from children's nursery rhymes to William Butler Yeats' Minnaloushe who danced by moonlight.

And there is no need to worry about the future; advertisements for the hit Broadway musical boldly proclaim: "Cats—Now and Forever."

POETRY, PROSE AND
NURSERY RHYMES ABOUT CATS

I like little Pussy, her coat is so warm,
And if I don't hurt her she'll do me
*   no harm;*
So I'll not pull her tail, nor drive
*   her away,*
But Pussy and I very gently will play.

SOURCE UNKNOWN

Ding, dong, bell,
Pussy's in the well;
Who put her in?
Little Tommy Green,
Who pulled her out?
Little Johnny Stout.

NURSERY RHYME

As I was going to St. Ives,
I met a man with seven wives,
Each wife had seven sacks,
Each sack had seven cats,
Each cat had seven kits:
Kits, cats, sacks, and wives,
How many were there going to St. Ives?

NURSERY RHYME

Sing, sing,
What shall I sing?
The cat's run away
With the pudding string!
Do, do,
What shall I do?
The cat's run away
With the pudding too!

NURSERY RHYME

When the tea is brought at five o'clock,
And all the neat curtains are drawn
 with care,
The little black cat with bright green eyes
Is suddenly purring there.

HAROLD MONRO,
Milk for the Cat

Dame Trot and her cat
Sat down for a chat;
The Dame sat on this side
And puss sat on that.

Puss, says the Dame,
Can you catch a rat,
Or a mouse in the dark?
Purr, says the cat.

NURSERY RHYME

Pussy cat, pussy cat,
Where have you been?
I've been to London
To visit the queen.
Pussy cat, pussy cat,
What did you there?
I frightened a little mouse
Under her chair.

NURSERY RHYME

There was a young lady of Riga,
Who went for a ride on a tiger;
They returned from the ride
With the lady inside,
And a smile on the face of the tiger.

ANONYMOUS

*Poor Matthias! Would'st thou have
More than pity? claim'st a stave!
—Friends more near us than a bird
We dismissed without a word,
Rover, with the good brown head,
Great Atossa, they are dead;
Dead, and neither prose nor rhyme
Tells the praises of their prime.
Thou did'st know them old and grey,
Knew them in their sad decay.
Thou hast seen Atossa sage
Sit for hours beside thy cage;
Thou would'st chirp, thou foolish bird,
Flutter, chirp—she never stirr'd!
What were now these toys to her?
Down she sank amid her fur;
Eyed thee with a soul resign'd—
And thou deemedst cats were kind!
—Cruel, but composed and bland,
Dumb, inscrutable and grand,
So Tiberius might have sat,
Had Tiberius been a cat.*

MATTHEW ARNOLD,
Poor Matthias

Hey diddle diddle,
The cat and the fiddle,
The cow jumped over the moon;
The little dog laughed
To see such sport,
And the dish ran away with the spoon.

MOTHER GOOSE

THE OWL
AND THE PUSSY-CAT

*T*HE OWL AND THE PUSSY-CAT
went to sea
 In a beautiful pea-green boat:
They took some honey, and plenty of
money
 Wrapped up in a five-pound note.
The Owl looked up to the stars above,
 And sang to a small guitar,
"O lovely Pussy, O Pussy, my love,
 What a beautiful Pussy you are,
   You are,
   You are!
 What a beautiful Pussy you are!"

Pussy said to the Owl, "You elegant
fowl,
 How charmingly sweet you sing!
Oh! let us be married; too long we
have tarried:
 But what shall we do for a ring?"
They sailed away, for a year and a day,
 To the land where the bong-tree
 grows;

And there in a wood a Piggy-wig stood,
  With a ring at the end of his nose,
      His nose,
      His nose,
  With a ring at the end of his nose.

"Dear Pig, are you willing to sell for
one shilling
  Your ring?" Said the Piggy, "I will."
So they took it away, and were
married next day
  By the Turkey who lives on the hill.
They dined on mince and slices of
quince,
  Which they ate with a runcible
  spoon;
And hand in hand, on the edge of the
sand,
  They danced by the light of the
  moon,
      The moon,
      The moon,
  They danced by the light of the
  moon.

EDWARD LEAR

SONNET TO
MRS. REYNOLD'S CAT

Cat, who has passed the grand
climacteric,
How many mice and rats hast in thy
days
Destroyed? How many titbits stolen?
Gaze
With those bright languid segments
green, and prick
Those velvet ears—but prithee do not
stick
Thy latent claws in me—and upraise
Thy gentle mew—and tell me all thy
frays
Of fish and mice and rats and tender
chicks.
Nay, look not down, nor lick thy
dainty wrists.
For all the wheezy asthma, and for all
Thy tail's tip is nicked off, and though
the fists
Of many a maid have given thee many
a maul.
      Still is thy fur as when the lists
In youth thou enterd'st on glass-
bottled wall.

JOHN KEATS

THE MASTER'S CAT

One evening we were all, except father, going to a ball, and when we started, we left "the master" and his cat in the drawing-room together. "The Master" was reading at a small table; suddenly the candle went out. My father, who was much interested in his book, relighted the candle, stroked the cat, who was looking at him pathetically he noticed, and continued his reading. A few minutes later, as the light became dim, he looked up just in time to see puss deliberately put out the candle with his paw, and then look appealingly at him. This second and unmistakable hint was not disregarded and puss was given the petting he craved.

CHARLES DICKENS' DAUGHTER MARY,
My Father as I Recall Him

THE CAT THAT
WALKED BY HIMSELF

*N*ext day the Cat waited to see if any other Wild Thing would go up to the Cave, but no one moved in the Wet Wild Woods, so the Cat walked there by himself; and he saw the Woman milking the Cow, and he saw the light of the fire in the Cave, and he smelt the smell of the warm white milk.

Cat said, "O my Enemy and Wife of my Enemy, where did Wild Cow go?"

The Woman laughed and said, "Wild Thing out of the Wild Woods, go back to the Woods again, for I have braided up my hair, and I have put away the magic blade-bone, and we have no more need of either friends or servants in our Cave."

Cat said, "I am not a friend, and I am not a servant. I am the Cat who walks by himself, and I wish to come into your Cave."

Woman said, "Then why did you not come with First Friend on the first night?"

Cat grew very angry and said, "Has Wild Dog told tales of me?"

Then the Woman laughed and said, "You are the Cat who walks by himself, and all places are alike to you. You are neither a friend nor a servant. You have said it yourself. Go away and walk by yourself in all places alike."

Then Cat pretended to be sorry and said, "Must I never come into the Cave? Must I never sit by the warm fire? Must I never drink the warm white milk? You are very wise and very beautiful. You should not be cruel even to a Cat."

Woman said, "I knew I was wise, but I did not know I was beautiful. So I will make a bargain with you. If ever I say one word in your praise, you may come into the Cave."

"And if you say two words in my praise?" said the Cat.

"I never shall," said the Woman, "but if I say two words in your praise, you may sit by the fire in the Cave."

"And if you say three words?" said the Cat.

"I never shall," said the Woman, "but if I say three words in your praise, you may drink the warm white milk three times a day for always and always and always."

Then the Cat arched his back and said, "Now let the Curtain at the mouth of the Cave, and the Fire at the back of the Cave, and the Milk-pots that stand beside the Fire, remember what my Enemy and the Wife of my Enemy has said." And he went away through the Wet Wild Woods waving his wild tail and walking by his wild lone.

RUDYARD KIPLING

THE HEN & THE CAT

A sly Cat, who had caught more than one chick in her day, hearing that a Hen was laid up sick in her nest, paid her a visit of condolence. She crept up to the nest and said softly: How are you, my dear friend? what can I do for you? what are you in want of? only tell me, if there is anything in the world that I can bring you. But you must keep up your spirits, and don't be alarmed. Thank you, said the Hen; but if you will be good enough to leave me alone, and ask your sisters to do likewise, I have no doubt but I shall soon be well enough. *The good wishes of an enemy make the wise man nervous.*

AESOP

THE QUOTABLE CAT

*W*e've got a cat called Ben
Hur. We called it Ben 'til it
had kittens.

SALLY POPLIN

*B*alanchine has trained his
cat to perform brilliant *jetés*
and *tours en l'air;* he says that
at last he has a body worth
choreographing for.

BERNARD TAPER

*E*very dog has its day, but
the nights are reserved for the
cats.

ANONYMOUS

*I*t's easy to understand why the cat has eclipsed the dog as modern America's favorite pet. People like pets to possess the same qualities they do. Cats are irresponsible and recognize no authority, yet are completely dependent on others for their material needs. Cats cannot be made to do anything useful. . . . In fact, cats possess so many of the same qualities as some people . . . that it's often hard to tell the people and the cats apart.

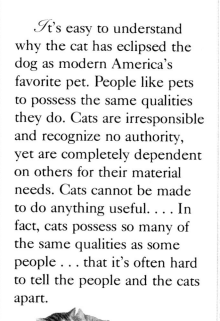

P. J. O'ROURKE,
Modern Manners

Cats, like men, are flatterers.

WALTER SAVAGE LANDOR

When a cat is alone she never purrs.

SAMUEL JOHNSON

Cats are intended to teach us that not everything in nature has a function.

GARRISON KEILLOR

*I*f a cat spoke, it would say things like "Hey, I don't see the *problem* here."

ROY BLOUNT, JR.

*C*at: a pygmy lion who loves mice, hates dogs, and patronizes human beings.

OLIVER HERFORD

A cat cares for you only as a source of food, security and a place in the sun. Her high self-sufficiency is her charm.

CHARLES HORTON COOLEY

*I*t would be a very good thing for the cat occasionally to find itself chased by the mouse.

ANTHONY BERKELEY

However superior to any number of cats a mouse may feel in its own hole, it requires a good deal of self-suggestion to maintain this opinion in the presence of the cat.

ANTHONY BERKELEY

It has been the providence of Nature to give this creature nine lives.

PILPAY

It is a very inconvenient habit of kittens (Alice had once made the remark) that, whatever you say to them, they *always* purr.

LEWIS CARROLL,
Through the Looking-Glass

*W*e tie bright ribbons around their necks, and occasionally little tinkling bells, and we affect to think that they are as sweet and vapid as the coy name "kitty" by which we call them would imply. It is a curious illusion. For, purring beside our fireplaces and pattering along our back fences, we have got a wild beast as uncowed and uncorrupted as any under heaven.

ALAN DEVOE

They say that the test (of literary power) is whether a man can write an inscription. I say, can he name a kitten. And by this test, I am condemned, for I cannot.

SAMUEL BUTLER

Cats are such good friends—they ask no questions, they accept no criticisms.

EDNA BEILENSON

I will admit to feeling exceedingly proud when any cat has singled me out for notice; for, of course, every cat is really the most beautiful woman in the room. That is part of their deadly fascination.

E. V. LUCAS

$\mathcal{A}$ baited cat may grow as
fierce as a lion.

SAMUEL PALMER

$\mathcal{B}$y associating with the
cat one only risks becoming
richer.

COLETTE

Are cats lazy? Well, more power to them if they are. Which one of us has not entertained the dream of doing just as he likes, when and how he likes, and as much as he likes?

FERNAND MERY

If a fish is the movement of water embodied, given shape, then cat is a diagram and pattern of subtle air.

DORIS LESSING